T0095149

BRASS TACKS
Christianity and Beyond!

ROGER L. BRADLEY

/

Order this book online at www.trafford.com
or email orders@trafford.com

Most Trafford titles are also available at major online book retailers.

© Copyright 2011 Roger L. Bradley.
All rights reserved. No part of this publication may be reproduced, stored in a retrieval
system, or transmitted, in any form or by any means, electronic, mechanical, photocopying,
recording, or otherwise, without the written prior permission of the author.

Printed in the United States of America.

ISBN: 978-1-4269-5171-8 (sc)
ISBN: 978-1-4269-5172-5 (hc)
ISBN: 978-1-4669-4683-5 (e)

Library of Congress Control Number: 2010918392

Trafford rev. 01/24/2011

 www.trafford.com

North America & International
toll-free: 1 888 232 4444 (USA & Canada)
phone: 250 383 6864 ♦ fax: 812 355 4082

DEDICATION

This book is dedicated to the Bradley family in which I grew up and which formed the context in which I learned a lot about life and the value of family nurturance. Whitney L. Bradley, Sr. and Lorena Y. Bradley successfully raised a family of eight children during the hardest of times, which included the great depression and over the span of four major wars. Both are now deceased; all but one of their children is still living at the time of this writing. My three sisters, Mary Messer, Laurie Brown and Bertha Welch are three living treasures and they have given me an army of nieces and nephews, all of whom are making their own mark in this world. Each of my four brothers has proven to be a real inspiration to me in a number of ways. Whitney Junior, who served in the USAF during WW II, is the patriarch of the family and has always set a great example of living by character and principle all through his life even as he approaches his 91st birthday. Wallace, now deceased, served in the US Army in the Italian Theater during WW II, and was the brother whose loving and faithful devotion to Christ became the instrument that led me to receiving Jesus Christ as my Lord and Savior at the age of 13. Richard, third older brother, was a career Noncommissioned Officer in the US Army and served in WW II, Korean and Vietnam wars. It is by his deep love of the Lord Jesus, diligent pursuit of Christian living, his insatiable hunger for the Word of God and anything that illumines that Scripture that I have been persuaded to publish this book. Finally, my brother, David, has served in the US Navy during the Korean War, and has been an inspiration by his diligence and loyalty in raising his family as a single parent after losing his loving wife to illness many years ago. His many acts of loving concern to his own children and his reaching out to give support and help to different members of the family in their times of need, never done to be noticed by others, has surely not escaped the watchful eye of our Lord. This book is also dedicated to my two children, Rosalyn and Peter, who are the joy and support of my life. They have been the objects of my constant admiration as they have faced and wrestled with many of life's challenges and have been succeeding— mainly because their faith and trust has been firmly placed in the Lord Jesus Christ. Their love for Jesus has been deep and constant; their commitment to Him fervent and steadfast. I know a crown of righteousness is in store for both of them when they pass into Glory.

CONTENTS